FACT FRENZY
SPACE

ASTEROIDS
AND COMETS

Lisa Regan

PowerKiDS
press

Published in 2021 by
The Rosen Publishing Group, Inc.
29 East 21st Street, New York, NY 10010

Cataloging-in-Publication Data
Names: Regan, Lisa.
Title: Asteroids and comets / Lisa Regan.
Description: New York : PowerKids Press, 2021. | Series:
Fact frenzy: space| Includes glossary and index.
Identifiers: ISBN 9781725320284 (pbk.) | ISBN
9781725320307 (library bound) | ISBN 9781725320291
(6 pack)
Subjects: LCSH: Asteroids--Juvenile literature. | Comets--
Juvenile literature.
Classification: LCC QB651.R465 2021 | DDC 523.44--dc23

Copyright © Arcturus Holdings Ltd, 2021

Manufactured in the United States of America

CPSIA Compliance Information: Batch CSPK20: For Further Information contact Rosen
Publishing, New York, New York at 1-800-237-9932.

Find us on

Contents

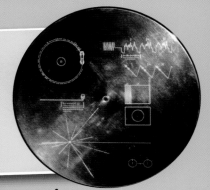

FLYING THROUGH THE ASTEROID BELT IS EASY

Movies and TV shows often show spacecraft struggling to fly through areas with lots of asteroids, dodging between huge, speeding rocks. The reality is much less exciting.

Asteroid belt

Asteroids are rocky objects—leftover bits and pieces from when the solar system formed billions of years ago—that still circle around the sun. In our solar system, between the planets Mars and Jupiter, there is an area of space containing millions of asteroids. This is known as the asteroid belt, and most of the asteroids in our solar system are found within it.

Saturn

Jupiter

Asteroid belt

Mars

Earth

Venus

What?!
I was expecting
a challenge!

Space between

Although there are lots of asteroids to avoid, there is typically around 620,000 to 1.8 million miles (1 to 2.9 million km) between each one. It's difficult to even get close enough to an asteroid to see it as you're flying through the belt, let alone having to constantly dodge around them! You really have to aim at a particular asteroid in order to be sure of seeing one.

This is a disappointingly boring flight.

Not all alike

The largest known asteroid, Vesta, is 359 miles (578 km) wide, although most are much smaller than this. Asteroids are made of rock and metal, and the different types and amounts of the materials that make them up change how they look. For example, asteroids that contain lots of metal are shiny.

Beyond the belt

Although most of the asteroids in our solar system are found in the asteroid belt, there are some in other areas, too. For instance, Trojans are what we call asteroids that circle around Jupiter. A number of asteroids pass close to Earth, and are known (a bit unimaginatively) as Near-Earth Asteroids. The ones that might be dangerous for Earth are the "Earth-crossers," asteroids that actually cross Earth's path and thus could crash into us!

COMETS ARE DIRTY SPACE SNOWBALLS

A comet is made of a mixture of frozen gases and ice, with bits of rock and dust stuck in it. These materials come from the time when our solar system was formed.

Gas tail

Dust tail

Icy core

Who are you calling a dirty space snowball?

Two tails

Comets are made up of an icy core and a trailing tail. In fact, most comets have one blue tail made of gas and another brighter tail made of dust. It is the sun's light hitting the dust particles in this tail that makes it shine so brightly. As the comet moves closer to the sun, the sunlight pushes these dust particles back away into a long tail that can stretch for almost 6 million miles (10 million km).

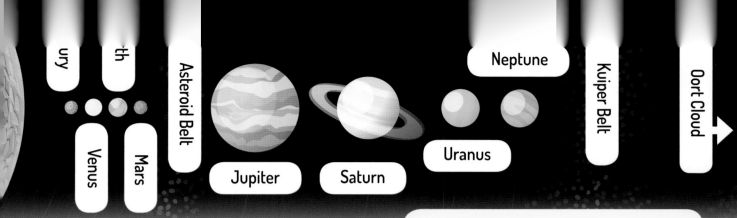

ury | th | Asteroid Belt | Jupiter | Saturn | Uranus | Neptune | Kuiper Belt | Oort Cloud

Venus | Mars

The Kuiper Belt

Comets in our solar system come from one of two places—the nearest one to us is the Kuiper Belt. This is a huge, disc-shaped area that begins close to Neptune and continues past Pluto, containing many different icy objects. The comets that come from the Kuiper Belt are short-period comets, which take less than 200 years to circle around the sun.

The Oort cloud

The Oort cloud is around 100 times farther away than the Kuiper Belt, running all around the edge of our solar system like a giant shell. No one knows for sure how many objects there are in the Oort cloud, but it may be around 2 trillion—around 266 times as many people on Earth. Scientists think that long-period comets, which take longer than 200 years to circle around the sun, come from this area.

Star finales

The most famous comet (for people on our planet, at least!) is Halley's Comet. It takes around 75 years to circle all the way around the sun, and we can only see it at one certain point in this journey. Seeing the comet is a once-in-a-lifetime event for all but the very luckiest people. It was last visible from Earth in 1986 and may be able to be seen again in 2061. Don't miss it!

A photo of Halley's Comet, taken in 1910.

I've been waiting for years to see this comet!

ASTEROIDS CAN HAVE THEIR OWN MOONS

Some of the bigger asteroids in our solar system have moons of their own. In 1993, a tiny moon was spotted for the first time circling the asteroid 243 Ida.

Hi, Galileo, I'm 243 Ida and this is my moon, Dactyl!

Dactyl

The name of 243 Ida's moon is Dactyl. It is only 1 mile (1.6 km) across, almost 20 times smaller than the asteroid. Dactyl moves quite slowly, circling 243 Ida at around 22 miles (36 km) per hour, which is only a bit faster than a person sprinting. Although Dactyl is pretty small and slow, it's still an impressive record breaker—the first moon of an asteroid ever discovered and photographed.

Galileo spacecraft

Dactyl was discovered by the Galileo space mission in 1993. The Galileo spacecraft was launched—with no one aboard—in 1989. It was the first spacecraft to explore Jupiter and its moons for a long period of time, circling around Jupiter for eight years. It took many pictures and measurements, teaching us more about this huge planet and its moons, but it also studied and photographed asteroids.

Not so special

Since this first sighting of an asteroid with a moon circling around it, scientists have discovered several more asteroids in our solar system that also have moons. In total, we know of more than 200 asteroids—both within and beyond our solar system—that have moons. In fact, there are asteroids that have more than one moon. A huge asteroid called 3122 Florence, which came pretty close to Earth in 2017, has two moons.

Scientists think that Jupiter has at least 79 moons!

Dwarf planets

We know that some planets have moons, and that asteroids can too, but what about another player in our solar system—dwarf planets? Well, Pluto may have been downgraded from a planet to a dwarf planet in 2006, but of the dwarf planets it is both the biggest and has the most moons—five! Haumea has two, Eris and Makemake each have one, and Ceres—which lies in the asteroid belt between Mars and Jupiter—doesn't have a moon.

PLUTO, 5 moons

HAUMEA, 2 moons

MAKEMAKE, 1 moon

ERIS, 1 moon

CERES, 0 moons

FACT 4 — EARTH DESTROYS A CAR-SIZED ASTEROID EVERY YEAR

About once a year, an asteroid the size of a car hits Earth's atmosphere—the mix of gases that surrounds our planet. This creates an impressive fireball, which burns up before reaching Earth's surface.

50 rhinos a day

Every day, more than 100 tons of material—roughly the combined weight of 50 rhinos—falls from space toward us. Although this is a lot of material, the individual pieces aren't normally very big. In fact, it is largely space dust and objects smaller than a grain of sand. Most of it burns up as it enters Earth's atmosphere.

Wheeeee!

FACT 5

Asteroids aren't that big, in space terms. If you rolled together all the asteroids known in our solar system, they would only make up 4% of the moon.

Burning up

When objects travel through space, they can reach very high speeds. When they hit Earth's atmosphere at this speed, they squash the gas particles in the atmosphere in front of them as they go. A gas that gets squashed like this gets hotter. This makes the object heat up too, until it gets so hot that it burns up.

Shuttle safety

When spacecraft return to Earth from space, they obviously have to reenter our planet's atmosphere. So why don't they burn up like the other objects falling to Earth from space? Well, if we're not very careful, they do. Obviously we don't want that—especially if there are people on board. Spacecraft either have special insulating tiles to stop them from getting too hot, or have a heat shield designed to melt away and carry off the heat.

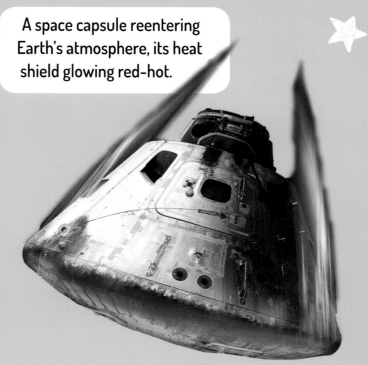

A space capsule reentering Earth's atmosphere, its heat shield glowing red-hot.

Danger from beyond

Some objects are big enough that they burn up a bit when they hit Earth's atmosphere, but not entirely. Usually the remains that hit Earth are very small and don't cause a problem. But if an asteroid more than 0.6 mile (1 km) wide hit Earth's atmosphere, it could have a global impact. There are asteroids in our solar system big enough to wipe out life on Earth, but they are too far away to be a danger.

An asteroid? Yikes!

SHOOTING STARS ARE NOT STARS AT ALL

Meteors are often called "shooting stars" because they look like bright stars moving across the sky, but they are not stars at all.

Not a star

A star appears as a still point of light in the night sky, and a meteor appears as a fast-moving streak of light. But although a meteor looks like a speeding star, they are actually very different. A star is a huge ball of burning gas far off in space, whereas a meteor is the glowing path of a small piece of rock or other matter that has entered Earth's atmosphere from space.

It's so beautiful ...

Yeah, not bad for a load of rocks and gas balls.

Burning bright

This small piece of rock or other matter from space, usually between the size of a grain of sand and a boulder, is called a meteoroid. When it hits Earth's atmosphere, it gets so hot that it burns up and changes into a gas. This burning gives off light, like a fire does, and we can see its visible path across the sky as a bright, glowing streak—which we call a meteor.

Meteoroids, meteors, meteorites?

So now that we know that a meteoroid is an object and a meteor is the light that it gives off as it burns up, let's look at meteorites ... Basically, if any part of an object from space makes it down to Earth's surface without burning up entirely in its atmosphere, it's a meteorite! It can be the leftover part of a meteoroid, an asteroid (which is bigger), or a comet (which is icy).

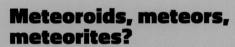

Meteorites found on Earth

Meteor showers

If you've ever been lucky enough to see a meteor, you'll know how special it feels to watch it zipping across the sky. Now imagine if you could see 100 of them in an hour! Meteor showers happen when lots of small objects fall into Earth's atmosphere at once, meaning that for a certain length of time—usually several days—there are lots more meteors to spot than normal.

FACT 7

Meteor showers that are especially intense are called meteor storms. During these events, you could see more than 1,000 meteors in an hour!

SCIENTISTS LANDED A SPACECRAFT ON A COMET

In 2016, for the very first time ever, a team of scientists managed to successfully land on the surface of a speeding comet. That's some careful driving!

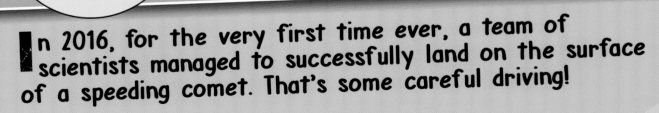

Can't you stay still for a second?! This is really hard!

Rosetta, Philae, and the comet

The landing craft that actually touched down on the comet was called Philae, and it was part of Rosetta, a larger spacecraft that had been following the comet for around two years. Rosetta launched in 2004, but it took 10 years to arrive at its target comet. This comet, called 67P/Churyumov–Gerasimenko, is named after the two scientists who first discovered it in 1969.

FACT 9

Earth was often hit by comets early in its life, and scientists believe they may have given us some of the water for our oceans.

Moving target

67P/Churyumov-Gerasimenko is around 2.5 miles (4 km) across, which sounds quite big, but as it travels at up to 84,000 miles (35,000 km) an hour, it's not an easy target on which to land! Imagine it by thinking of trying to land on an area the length of Central Park in New York, while Central Park is moving at more than 300 times the speed of the fastest car in the world.

Bumpy landing

As Philae dropped down toward the comet, it took close-up photographs to help scientists understand more about comets. Unfortunately, Philae's landing wasn't a smooth one—it bounced twice and ended up in a shadowy area, where its solar batteries couldn't get enough light to charge up properly. In July 2015, as the comet passed near the sun, the batteries recharged and the lander restarted, but it soon ran out of power once more.

Philae landing craft.

Mission end

The Philae lander is still attached to the comet, and scientists hope that it may still send back more photos in the future. For the Rosetta spacecraft, however, the end came in September 2016 when it crash-landed into the comet. This was a planned end to the mission, as the comet is heading out into the outer reaches of our solar system. There isn't enough sunlight out there to continue powering Rosetta to fly through space with it.

That comet can't hurt me now!

FACT 10

In 1910, Earth passed through the tail of a comet. Some people were so scared about its possible effects that they bought "anti-comet" umbrellas!

HUMANS ARE LEAVING JUNK IN SPACE

There are more than 17,000 artificial objects circling around Earth—and these are only the ones large enough to be tracked.

Bits and pieces

We think there are around 170 million smaller pieces of space junk, too, from paint flakes to nuts and bolts. Even the very tiniest objects can damage spacecraft. Bigger objects can be very dangerous if spacecraft crash into them because they are moving so fast—faster than a speeding bullet—as they circle around Earth.

Come on, guys, clean up after yourselves!

No longer needed

There are more than 1,400 working satellites circling around Earth, but there are also lots of old satellites that aren't in use anymore. There are many pieces of burned-out equipment used to launch missions into space, left behind after over 60 years of space exploration. There is a risk of this space junk crashing into working satellites and damaging them.

Chain reaction

Every time pieces of space junk crash into each other, more bits can break off and increase the total number of unwanted objects floating around Earth. If objects have any leftover fuel or batteries, they may also explode and send out lots of smaller bits. The only way to control the amount of junk circling around Earth is to remove the larger items.

One of the many satellites circling Earth.

Clearing up

RemoveDebris is a small, experimental satellite sent out into space to try out clearing up some of this space junk. In 2018, it caught its first piece in a test run—it sent out a target, which it then recaptured in a net, and the satellite and space junk fell back to Earth to burn up in the atmosphere. A net seems like a strangely simple idea, but it seems to do the job!

Space junk crashing into the International Space Station could be very dangerous for the astronauts on board.

MOST METEORITES ARE SMALLER THAN AN ORANGE

Every day, tons of meteorites reach Earth's surface. But don't worry too much about getting hit by one on its way down—each one is usually tiny, no more than a speck of dust!

What is a meteorite?

A meteorite is an object that has come from space and crossed through Earth's atmosphere, before landing somewhere on its surface. It was originally part of a larger (but still relatively small) object, which burned up as it hit Earth's atmosphere until only this small bit remained. This larger object may itself be a broken-off piece of an asteroid or a comet.

The orange looks tastier!

FACT 13

Meteorites have been spotted on the surface of Mars and other planets.

20

A meteorite falling into the ocean.

Where do they land?

Over 70% of Earth's surface is covered in water, so it makes sense that most meteorites end up landing in water rather than on land. They fall randomly all over the world, but it is easiest to spot and collect the ones that have landed in desert areas—both hot, sandy deserts and cold, snowy areas such as Antarctica.

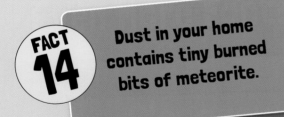

FACT
14
Dust in your home contains tiny burned bits of meteorite.

Not just meteorites

Asteroids and comets can also crash-land on our planet's surface. Like meteorites, they will partly burn up as they pass through Earth's atmosphere, but what survives and hits Earth can be much bigger than any meteorite. This means that they can create much bigger craters, and even have a worldwide impact—scientists believe an asteroid hitting Earth led to the dinosaurs dying out.

Crashes and craters

If a meteorite is big enough, it creates a visible crater when it crash-lands. A crater is a bowl-shaped dip in the ground, with a raised ring around its top edge. There are fewer than 200 impact craters on Earth, but the moon has thousands all over its surface. Earth's atmosphere slows down and burns up falling objects, but the moon gets the full impact of any crash landing.

This impact crater was made almost 50,000 years ago.

WE HAVE SENT OUT MESSAGES FOR ALIENS

The Voyager I spacecraft was launched in 1977 with a solid gold record on board. It plays sounds from Earth and is intended as a friendly introduction for aliens who find it.

Introducing Earth

If you had to introduce an alien to life on Earth, which sights and sounds would you choose to give them the best possible understanding of our planet? The people responsible for the Golden Record had to decide exactly this. No pressure! A committee put together by NASA and headed by famous scientist Carl Sagan worked together to choose the contents—a selection of images, music, sounds from Earth, and greetings in different languages.

FACT 16

The Golden Record has a recording of a woman's brainwaves as she thought about subjects including history, Earth's problems, and what it is like to fall in love.

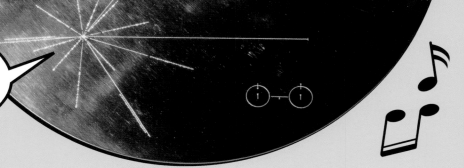

Hello! We are from Earth!

Wie gehts?

Cover art

The record cover has a number of diagrams on one side, explaining where the spacecraft comes from and how the record can be played. As you would hope, NASA thought to include a record player on board so that any aliens can actually play it! There are also 115 images encoded onto the record itself—including photos of a city at night, heavy traffic on a road, and people eating or drinking in different ways.

One of the images on the Golden Record, showing people eating and drinking— a bit strangely!

THE GOLDEN RECORD IS DESIGNED TO STILL BE PLAYABLE A BILLION YEARS FROM NOW.

Earth sounds

Aliens playing the record will first hear a number of human greetings—starting in an ancient language called Akkadian and finishing in a modern Chinese dialect called Wu. The sounds of Earth include a human heartbeat, a baby crying, a train, and a dog barking. After this comes a 90-minute selection of music from all over the world— including classical Western and Eastern music, traditional songs from indigenous communities, rock 'n' roll, and the blues.

Swinging through space

The Voyager I (left) and Voyager II spacecraft were launched in the 1970s to take advantage of planets in our solar system lining up in a way that only happens every 176 years. The spacecraft used the gravity of each planet to swing to the next and eventually study our solar system's outer planets. After leaving our solar system, they will travel through mostly empty space for a very long time—but we hope aliens may come across them someday ...

TOYS ARE FLYING THROUGH SPACE RIGHT NOW

When NASA launched the Juno spacecraft in 2011, there were three special guests on board... They are circling around Jupiter, farther away from Earth than any human has ever been.

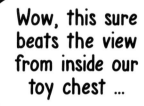

Hi-tech toys

These space explorers aren't your average toys. They are LEGO® figures made entirely from a special type of space-grade metal that has been tested to make sure it won't interfere with anything on board. The trio are models of the ancient Roman god Jupiter, his wife Juno, and the scientist Galileo Galilei—who discovered the four largest moons of Jupiter.

Wow, this sure beats the view from inside our toy chest ...

Juno and Jupiter

The Juno spacecraft is on a mission to explore Jupiter and bring back more information about the largest planet in our solar system. It is hoped that this new knowledge will help scientists further develop ideas about the creation of giant planets and of our solar system. The onboard crew of three also has a further mission—to get more children interested in space travel.

Galileo Galilei

Ancient Romans thought Jupiter and Juno ruled over the other gods and goddesses.

The planet Jupiter and the Juno spacecraft circling around it.

Toys in space

These three special passengers aren't the first toys to go into space—several toys have been flown up to the International Space Station. Buzz Lightyear, from the movie *Toy Story*, has also spent 450 days in space, including a year aboard the International Space Station.

Along for the ride

As well as toys, there have been a number of interesting objects launched into space over the years. In 2018, billionaire Elon Musk launched a sports car into space aboard a rocket, and it is still speeding through our solar system.

EVEN MORE FACTS!

You've found out lots about asteroids and comets, but there's always more to discover! Boost your knowledge here with even more facts.

In 2011, the Dawn spacecraft traveled to the asteroid belt to study Vesta, the largest asteroid. A year later, Dawn left to orbit the largest object in the asteroid belt, the dwarf planet Ceres.

Ceres is so big that it is categorized as a dwarf planet. Ceres is 597 miles (961 km) in diameter and contains one-third of the total mass of the asteroid belt.

Scientists estimate there are over 1 million asteroids with a diameter over 0.6 mile (1 km) in the asteroid belt. The five largest asteroids make up over half the total mass of the asteroid belt.

A telescope called the Herschel Space Observatory has recently discovered that the Comet Hartley 2 has the same type of water as Earth's oceans, meaning it could be one of the sources of our oceans.

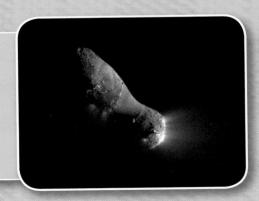

The Oort cloud is about one light-year from the sun. The outer limit of the Oort cloud defines the outer boundary of our solar system.

In the past, comets were thought of as bad omens. For instance, in 1066, Halley's Comet was seen over England a few months before William the Conqueror defeated King Harold II at the Battle of Hastings.

The name "comet" comes from the Greek word meaning "hair of the head," after the Greek philospopher Aristotle called comets "stars with hair."

Halley's Comet is named after the English astronomer Edmond Halley, who first identified it and predicted when it would reappear, correctly proving the length of its orbit.

Meteorites that are observed falling from space and are then collected are called "falls." All other meteorites are called "finds." There have been 1,000 collected falls and 40,000 finds to date.

When space stations wear out, to stop any debris from reaching the ground, they are planned to fall on a remote area in the Pacific Ocean, called the Spacecraft Cemetery.

ASTEROIDS AND COMETS GLOSSARY

asteroid A small, rocky object made up of material left over from the birth of the solar system.

asteroid belt A region between the orbits of Mars and Jupiter, containing a concentration of asteroids moving around the sun.

astronomer A scientist who studies the stars, planets, and other natural objects in space.

atmosphere A shell of gases kept around a planet, star, or other object by its gravity.

comet A chunk of rock and ice from the edge of the solar system.

core The central part of something.

crater A very large hole in the ground, created by something hitting it or by an explosion.

dwarf planet A world, orbiting a star, that looks like a planet but does not meet certain criteria needed to make it a true planet.

gravity A natural force created around objects with mass, which draws other objects toward them.

International Space Station (ISS) A space station launched in 1998 with the cooperation of 16 nations. The ISS orbits Earth for scientific and space research.

Kuiper Belt A ring of small icy worlds directly beyond the orbit of Neptune. Pluto is the largest known Kuiper Belt object.

landing craft In space, part of a spacecraft used to land on the surface of a planet or moon.

light-year The distance light travels in a year—about 5.9 trillion miles (9.5 trillion km).

meteor The glowing path of a small piece of rock or other matter that has entered Earth's atmosphere. It appears as a fast-moving streak of light in the night sky, and is also known as a "shooting star."

meteorite A large piece of rock or metal from space that has landed on Earth.

meteoroid A small rocky or metallic object moving through space.

moon Earth's closest companion in space, a ball of rock that orbits Earth every 27.3 days. Most other planets in the solar system have moons of their own.

NASA An abbreviation for "National Aeronautics and Space Administration," the American government organization concerned with spacecraft and space travel.

observatory A building or room that contains a telescope or other scientific equipment used to study space.

Oort cloud A spherical (ball-shaped) shell of sleeping comets, surrounding all of the solar system out to a distance of about two light-years.

orbit A fixed path taken by one object in space around another because of the effect of gravity.

particle A very small piece or part of something.

planet A world, orbiting a star, that has enough mass and gravity to pull itself into a ball-like shape, and clear space around it of other large objects.

rocket A vehicle that drives itself forward through a controlled chemical explosion and can therefore travel in the vacuum of space. Rockets are the only practical way to launch spacecraft and satellites.

satellite Any object orbiting a planet. Moons are natural satellites made of rock and ice. Artificial satellites are machines in orbit around Earth.

solar batteries Batteries that contain solar cells, which convert the energy of sunlight into electric power.

solar system The eight planets (including Earth) and their moons, and other objects such as asteroids, that orbit the sun.

spacecraft A vehicle that travels into space.

telescope A device that collects light or other radiations from space and uses them to create a bright, clear image. Telescopes can use either a lens or a mirror to collect light.

trillion A million million.

FURTHER INFORMATION

BOOKS

Aguilar, David. *Space Encyclopedia*. London, UK: National Geographic Kids, 2013.

Becklade, Sue. *Wild About Space*. Thaxted, UK: Miles Kelly, 2020.

Betts, Bruce. *Astronomy for Kids: How to Explore Outer Space with Binoculars, a Telescope, or Just Your Eyes!* Emeryville, CA: Rockridge Press, 2018.

DK. *The Astronomy Book: Big Ideas Simply Explained*. London, UK: DK, 2017.

DK. *Knowledge Encyclopedia Space!: The Universe as You've Never Seen It Before*. London, UK: DK, 2015.

Frith, Alex, Jerome Martin, and Alice James. *100 Things to Know About Space*. London, UK: Usborne Publishing, 2016.

National Geographic Kids. *Everything: Space*. London, UK: Collins, 2018.

WEBSITES

Ducksters Astronomy for Kids
http://www.ducksters.com/science/astronomy.php
Head to this website to find out all there is to know about astronomy; you can also try an astronomy crossword puzzle and word search!

NASA Science: Space Place
https://spaceplace.nasa.gov
Discover all sorts of facts about space, other planets, and the moon. You can even play the Mars Rover Game, sending commands to the Mars rover and collecting as much data as possible in eight expeditions!

Science Kids: Space for Kids
http://www.sciencekids.co.nz/space.html
Go beyond our planet and explore space through fun facts, games, videos, quizzes, and projects.

Publisher's note to educators and parents: Our editors have carefully reviewed these websites to ensure that they are suitable for students. Many websites change frequently, however, and we cannot guarantee that a site's future contents will continue to meet our high standards of quality and educational value. Be advised that students should be closely supervised whenever they access the Internet.

INDEX